Five Women

Five Women

Sarah, Hagar, Rebekah, Rachel, Leah

Christianne Méroz

Translated by Dennis Wienk

WIPF & STOCK · Eugene, Oregon

FIVE WOMEN
Sarah, Hagar, Rebekah, Rachel, Leah

Wipf & Stock
An Imprint of Wipf and Stock Publishers
199 W. 8th Ave., Suite 3
Eugene, OR 97401
www.wipfandstock.com

ISBN 13: 978-4-62032-154-6
Manufactured in the U.S.A.

Originally published in 1988 as *Des femmes libres*. Copyright ©
1988, Editions du Moulin SA, Ch-1170 Aubonne, Switzerland.
English translation copyright © 2012, Wipf and Stock Publishers,
Eugene, Oregon 97401 USA.

Contents

Acknowledgments

M Y THANKS AS TRANSLATOR go quickly to the Rev. Lawrence Crumb, associate professor emeritus, University of Oregon, who not only gave me the book originally, but also suggested the English title; to the author Christianne Méroz, whose desire to see her little book appear in English matched my own; and to my wife Marilyn Wienk, who shares my deep interest in the matriarchs and their families.

Introduction

USUALLY WHEN WE READ the biblical narratives of the ancestors of Israel, it is the role of the males, the patriarchs, that catches our attention right away. However, a more attentive reading soon reveals the presence of women who also have put their stamp, often much more indelibly than it might at first appear, on the destiny of the people of God. By analogy with the patriarchs, we will call these women the "matriarchs."

It is their lives that I propose to call forth in this little book, their personalities and their profound attitudes about God in the patriarchal society of their epoch. It will not be an exhaustive study, but I have tried to bring together enough material to give the reader a good working tool.

We can approach the lives of the matriarchs from the outside, searching the data we have bit by bit in order to penetrate the heart of their existence. But once we have done this, it still remains to try to express and appreciate the interior richness that is there. That is why I have chosen the midrashic* (words followed by an asterisk are explained in the lexicon at the end of this book) style as my method of analysis and expression. This way of grappling with the biblical text, related as it is more to poetry than to logic, does not however betray its truth.

In a concern for faithfulness that is more spiritual than literal, I have wanted to make the lives of the matriarchs and their experience of freedom truly live. Their experience is, on the one hand, bathed in the light of mercy and, on the other, darkened by the weight of patriarchal structures. These two aspects are certainly connected, but not to the point of totally stifling all autonomous behavior. Within the limits of a patriarchal society, it is possible for the reader of these narratives to discover some paths of freedom and to travel on those paths.

My intention here has been to make some openings, clear some lines of reflection, and exploit the materials in such a way that readers of both sexes will be able to enter into the study with me.

I have drawn widely from the Jewish tradition chiefly for two reasons. The first is that it seems normal and natural to me to seek to know better the richness of the tradition from which Christianity stems. The second is the hope that doing so will encourage Jewish and Christian women who possess these stories in common to meet together. As for the Islamic tradition, I have only touched its surface in treating Hagar. Perhaps these few remarks though will awaken the desire of some readers to know more about that tradition and will occasion exchanges that will lead to a greater mutual understanding among all communities.

one

Sarah and Hagar

Beauty as the Presence of God

SARAH, REBEKAH, RACHEL, AND Leah are the names of women that the Christian tradition, intentionally or not, has slighted. For numerous commentators they are only the shadows of their husbands. However, the promises of God depend on these women.

The whole patriarchal history is crisscrossed by the theme of procreation for the sake of the tribe's future to such a point that sterility is truly a curse. Therefore we must recognize that history devolves not only through the fathers, but likewise through the mothers. We possess a wealth of anecdotes and detail about the lives of Abraham, Isaac, and Jacob, but such is not the case with their wives. As for Hagar, whose role is essential, she has been almost totally eradicated from the Christian tradition.

Rashi* (1040–1105 CE), the famous commentator on the Torah,* compares the four Mothers of Israel with incense, so sweet is the fragrance of their lives to God and the whole human race, and even more particularly to us women who are discovering in them friends and confidants, as well as liberating role models.

As spouses of the patriarchs, the matriarchs each have a specific and determining part to play in the formation of the people of God. Their place is not only in the bosom of the patriarchal family but also at the core of history. God chose them as fulltime partners in the plan of salvation.

1. SARAH

Abram, son of Terah, was born in Ur of the Chaldees. It was in the region of Lower Mesopotamia that he met Sarai, whom tradition introduces to us as the daughter of the king of Haran. She became his wife, and immediately the Bible tells us that she is barren (Gen 11:30). This note might surprise us. It is not at all flattering for a woman to be from the outset presented by what was felt in the patriarchal society of the time to be an actual curse.

However, this mention of Sarai's sterility, negative though it might be, marks the beginning of personal history. Before her the few women mentioned in the Bible are only names, and sometimes even less than that. We know nothing, for example, of the wife of Noah. We are also provided with the detail that Sarai was of pagan origin, which inspires some commentators to say that it was necessary to make this gratuitous observation in order to highlight her radical break with the past.

Communion and Rupture

In marrying Abram, Sarai leaves her country and family to enter freely into a new life. This is clearly affirmed in the next verse, which tells us of the departure of the whole family of Terah for Canaan (Gen 11:31).

Abram experienced a similar demand for a rupture. After the death of his father Terah, God calls him and asks him to leave his country (Gen 12:1). When Sarai and then Abram willingly leave their social setting and their family affections, a love of adventure is not the motive. Rather they are doing it because they have understood that the fulfillment of their lives as a woman and as a man ineluctably involves a rupture. "Go on," God says, "to what I am calling you to become."

Abram hears, which means that he obeys. He accepts becoming a stranger in a strange land, a nomad. From then on, deprived of his identity as a citizen of Haran, he is received by God to become, according to the promise that is made to him, a great nation. Leaning on God's word alone, in complete ignorance of how it will be fulfilled in view of Sarai's sterility, Abram leaves with his wife and his nephew Lot for the country that God will show him.

One must have faith when risking one's own life and the lives of others in this way. But courage is necessary as well. Putting one's identity in jeopardy, following one's intuition, this is the behavior of people who are sure of themselves. In the case of Sarai and Abram, it really seems that it was the call of God, the divine disturber, that gives them courage and faith. This call in fact means that they have been chosen and loved by God. Therefore, we can imagine that this couple understands the imperative "go" as "come,"—"Come and follow me; enter a life of friendship with me." It is first an invitation to share life with God and only then a demand for a break with the past.

A Revolting Demand

Once settled in the land of Canaan, Abram and Sarai do not stay there long. Pushed on by famine, they emigrate to Egypt. Curiously it is in the course of this trip that fate snaps its fingers at the couple. It is only when they arrive in Egypt that Abram discovers his wife, discovers her beauty. This is, at the very least, an astonishing remark. How, after all these years of life together, has he only now noticed the great beauty of his wife? It is true that the text says, "I know" (Gen 12:11), and Rashi* adds, "I knew for a long time."

Perhaps this is true. But what interests us in this remark is that the unveiling of Sarai's face, of her beauty, of her femininity, provokes the first real dialogue in the Bible between a man and a woman. And this happens at the very moment when the couple's life is in danger. Abram fears for his own life. He is not ignorant of the custom of regional kings to take foreign widows or unmarried women into their harem. Sarai, we have learned, is a very beautiful woman. This is why Abram asks her to pretend she is his sister. This first dialogue therefore takes the form of a prayer, "Say you are my sister" (Gen 12:13), he begs.

Abram's request is worth a word of explanation. At this time in the countries of the East, an unmarried woman was better protected, so to speak, than a married woman. A married woman, especially if she was foreign, ran the risk of being taken away once her husband was killed. However, an unmarried woman, accompanied by her brother, became the bargaining chip between the brother and whoever coveted her.

Because of the customs of the time, Abram is really in danger. If we consider simply his point of view, we can understand his strange request. However, Abram is not alone in the affair, and the fate he proposes to Sarai is hardly more to be desired than his own. What woman would accept being handed over to male desire in exchange for a few camels?

What could have inspired Abram to propose such a solution? Perhaps it is the discovery of his wife's beauty, which suddenly appears to him not only as physical beauty but also as moral beauty, a great goodness. In the book of Proverbs it is written, "Say to wisdom, 'You are my sister'" (Prov 7:4). Wisdom, in Jewish tradition, is one of the names of God, and so Sarai's beauty becomes a sign of the divine presence for her husband. We can conclude that it was this revelation that emboldened him to tell this lie.

So Abram has thought it all out and planned his survival as best he can. At no moment, however, does he seem to have imagined the thing that actually happens. Pharaoh takes Sarai into his harem. From then on it is no longer a question of the so-called brother's requests. He has to be contented with what he gets. Pharaoh does not ask if Abram agrees about the price any more than Abram asked his wife if he might engage her in this ruse.

The Emergence of the Woman

This passage is astounding because of the role that Sarai plays in it. According to the text, she is silent from beginning to end. In her woman's heart, it seems, she knows that as a couple they are called to a destiny from which she cannot break away.

So the strange—most would say revolting—demand that is made of her, to become a gift to Pharaoh, represents a decisive turning point for Sarai, the moment to make an existential choice. In silence she accepts putting her husband's welfare ahead of her own. Without invoking her freedom, her dignity as a woman and wife, she finds herself, by her own choice, suddenly responsible for the life of her husband and of their posterity promised by God. In choosing to safeguard the life of the couple, and at the same time to put it in jeopardy, she enters wholly into the divine plan. And Sarai's beauty, which could have been a source of ambiguity, becomes by her goodness the source of life.

In tacitly consenting to become Abram's sister, Sarai puts herself resolutely on the level of her husband's equal and opposite number with all the creative richness of her otherness, her difference. Silently but freely, she takes the place of Abram. All the risks, all the humiliations, including some of the greatest ones, are part of her role. Like the image of the Suffering Servant of Isaiah 53, she sets out on the path of a choice that we can call "messianic." In fact the boldness of her love and compassion signifies a new way of living, a new way of being. She is not simply the shadow of her husband, the one who follows him without a word. Instead, she is the woman, the one through whom the other can live. By putting her own life and the life of the couple in jeopardy, she reveals that neither one of them can live without the other, that neither can live without giving herself or himself to the other.

Autonomous, yet in Solidarity

In accepting the divine invitation to walk with God and become a great people, Abram and Sarai find themselves engaged in a story that is infinitely bigger than they are. Both are very conscious that the fulfillment of the divine word rests with them as a couple. Just as they realize that they are responsible to God, however, so God is to them. This is why God intervenes and sends plagues on Pharaoh, and thanks to God's intervention, the couple can go on their way again (Gen 12:17–20).

The divine promise must have been a burden at times for this couple, advanced in age as they were, and still without a child. This is why when Sarai finally decides to ask her husband to take her slave Hagar to give him a son, Abram accepts without discussion and places the welfare of his wife ahead of his sadness at not having his firstborn from his chosen wife.

With the birth of Ishmael, we are present at the second human attempt on the part of Abram and Sarai to fulfill the divine promise. Again it is not God's solution. Once more God must intervene so that Sarai, having become Sarah (Gen 17:15), can finally give a son to Abraham, who has also changed his name (Gen 17:5). Both have to be marked in their flesh, by maternity and by circumcision, in order that God's word might be fulfilled.

One after the other, each having become responsible for the other, Sarah and Abraham show us the way of a spirituality of choice that, even though it implies a renunciation of self, can never be reduced to a simple submission to the desire of the other.

Because they knew how to watch over that part of themselves which was greater than they and which the Bible calls "the image of God," because they knew how to keep the word of God alive in them, because they respected in each other his or her otherness and difference, and because they kept themselves as a couple in dialogue with God and history, Sarah and Abraham became the parents of the child of the covenant.

At the beginning of the people of God then, we find a woman and a man who dare to make personal and messianic choices that reveal truly autonomous behavior. In order that the work of God might be accomplished, each one pursues her or his own way, but it is together that they realize it. Through their experiences of two personalities in dialogue, we see the emergence of a collaboration for good and for life. Respect for the mystery of the other permits a creative dialogue in which each can be fully herself or himself in a unique relation to God, to the other, and to others.

Fidelity to a personal choice in life saves them from the risk of being fettered by bonds in which one exists only by and for the other. True availability and compassion, it seems, must not be allowed to tyrannize over the self, for that would only amount to destroying one's own personality without profit to anyone. On the contrary, these traits must always be an epiphany, a revelation of the presence of the image of God.

Mother of Believers

Right up into our era Christian tradition has not given Sarah the place that belongs to her. Her husband Abraham is "the father of believers," "the father of the faithful." But who is she?

In the First Testament, however, the Bible tells us, "Look to Sarah who bore you" (Isa 51:2). This verse which introduces the songs of the Suffering Servant not only emphasizes the essential role of Sarah in the story of salvation, but authorizes us from that point on to join her name to Abraham's when, in the epistle to the Hebrews for example, mention is made of the patriarch's faith alone. Sarah's faith carries her not only through her sterility, but through all her acts, through all the moments of her life as woman and wife (Heb 11:11–12).

The Second Testament barely refers to Sarah. Abraham is mentioned seventy-seven times, but his wife only five times. First Peter gives her as a moral example and a model of conjugal submission (1 Pet 3:1–7). Paul is content simply in Romans to emphasize her sterility (Rom 4:19), and in Galatians to make an unconvincing allegory of the mother of the people of God (Gal 4:22–31).

Speaking of Paul's attitude, Jean Vanel writes, "Malleable to Paul's wants, in his hands Sarah loses all her consistency, all her value as a religious archetype, all her marvelous stature as a woman who is the source and mother and mirror of humanity, to become a cold allegory emptied of all her traditional symbolism. She was a female image of God, and she becomes an equation, an object. Paul uses her as a handy instrument, chosen from among biblical characters, to attain his personal ends. . . . Sarah in his hands is hardly more than a marionette; he uses her, but she does not interest him."

Today we can no longer simply let it be a contrast between two women, Sarah and Hagar, or even Isaac and Ishmael. In giving Sarah back her place as the "woman who is the source of humanity" in the history of the three monotheistic religions, we will certainly discover further paths of dialogue.

And Mary Took the Place of All . . .

For Christians a big reason for which Sarah has remained in a shadow has to do with the prominence of the role of Mary. For example, when we compare the different annunciation narratives, we find the same expressions (cf. Gen 17:19 and Luke 1:13; or Gen 16:11 and Luke 1:31). It is striking to note that in the cases of married couples such as Sarah and Abraham, or Elizabeth and Zachariah, the announcement of a child is made to the husband. By contrast, for Hagar and Mary, two single women, it is to them personally that the announcement of an approaching birth is made and to them also that the name of the child is confided. We can also emphasize the parallel between the reaction of Zachariah, "I am an old man" (Luke 1:18), and that of Sarah, "I have grown old" (Gen 18:12).

There is nothing in the biblical texts that justifies the scant interest that Sarah has met with among Christians. It appears that tradition has replaced the figure of Sarah with that of Mary. While Christians call Mary the new Eve, "to whom turn the faces of all who formerly were exiled from Paradise" (Romanos the Melodist), for Jews, as the Zohar* expresses it, "Sarah is the new Eve; Eve caused death in the world, whereas Sarah won eternal life for all her posterity."

Christians call Mary "spotless," and the Talmud* of Babylon says, "Sarah our mother was chaste." Mary conceived by the Holy Spirit, and "Sarah is inhabited by the Holy Spirit." Mary is without sin, and "Sarah at the age of one hundred was as innocent of sin as in her twentieth year," or as Rabbi Yo'hanan says more poetically, "She was as innocent as a young lamb." Even their names have the same meaning: Sarah means "princess," and Mary, Miriam in Aramaic, has the same sense. And finally, there is a similar experience in the suffering of the two women. Both Mary at the foot of the cross and Sarah at the time of the near sacrifice of Isaac endure grief as two equally brokenhearted mothers.

In Genesis history is made jointly by women and men, mothers and fathers, that is, history devolves in a similar fashion in the feminine and masculine spheres. In the prophets God becomes both father and mother—"I thought you would call me, my Father" (Jer 3:19), and Jeremiah also says, "I love them with a maternal and fruitful love" [(Jer 33:26) the author's translation; "I will restore their fortunes, and will have mercy on them" (NRSV)]. Isaiah uses the beautiful image of the mother who comforts and plays with her child on her knees (Isa 66:12–13; cf. Hos 11:3–4).

This image of a God who is both paternal and maternal disappears in the Second Testament. There it is Mary who receives the title of mother (John 19:27) and in whom all feminine characteristics are concentrated. This explains not only the virtual disappearance of the person of Sarah and the other matriarchs, but also the disappearance of woman as a person. The feminine element is completely erased from the image of God, with the resulting impoverishment. God is now only the almighty Father. With very few exceptions we have to wait until our own time and the appearance of the women's movement in order to rediscover the feminine and maternal aspects of God.

New Names

The Targum* of Jonathan tells us how Abram and Sarai had to cross a river in order to get into Egypt. They undress, and Abram then says to Sarai, "Up to now I had not looked at your body, but now I know that you are a beautiful woman."

To uncover the real face of Sarah, we must discern what hides behind her gestures, her words, her silences. We must read the shadow and light of her life; or to express it as the Jewish tradition does, the black, that which is written, and the white, that which is written between the lines. To understand Scripture well, we must read both.

We have already noted that Sarah's is not only a physical beauty but a moral beauty as well. She is in herself the sign of the presence of God. In her, beauty becomes goodness. She is productive of the good; she is the source of life. Sarah does not keep this presence of God jealously for herself; she gives half of it to her husband. Jewish tradition explains the change of name that takes place at the moment when the sterile Sarai becomes Sarah, the future mother of Isaac (Gen 17:15–16). This change of names is made by adding an "h" to the name of Abram who becomes Abraham, and for Sarai by replacing the last letter "i," in Hebrew "yod," with an "h" also, in Hebrew "hē." So by a change of name, Sarah permits God in some way to give Abraham a portion of the divine presence that was found in his wife. Furthermore, since the "hē" in Jewish mysticism symbolizes fertility, they can from now on be father and mother of the promised posterity.

Besides all this, the name Sarai, which means "my" princess, acquires a universal value when it is changed to Sarah, which means simply "princess." Thus Sarah is not first and foremost the wife-mother-procreator bound to Abraham; she is "princess for all" and has a role to play for all humanity (cf. Isa 51:2). This is the sense of the double benediction that God gives her after her change of name. "I will bless her, and moreover I will give you a son by her. I will bless her, and she shall give rise to nations; kings of peoples shall come from her" (Gen 17:16).

God gave new names, and from this time on there is a real change in both persons. Abraham and Sarah are marked by this change in their flesh, the one by circumcision, the other by maternity (Gen 17). The Midrash* even supposes that God would have given Sarah the ovary that she lacked. According to Rashi* Sarah recovers her youth; as it is mused, "Shall I have pleasure?" (Gen 18:12)

It is very difficult to pronounce on the youth or the age of Sarah. Moreover, it is important to note that Sarah seems to have a young heart throughout her life, making her 127 years a succession of renewals of life.

Reading the "white" as well as the "black" of the biblical text, we see little by little that she is an autonomous woman who appears with her own joys, her own pains, her own fights and shadows and lights. Sarah has a separate existence from that of her husband; she is a respected woman who is listened to (Gen 21:12). An equal to her husband, she is really his counterpart. And in fulfillment of the divine promise, both have a role to play, neither surpassing the other. This is surely the meaning of the Hebrew text of the narrative of the birth of Isaac where we find Sarah's name six times and Abraham's name six times (Gen 21:1–8). On top of that, in the second story of the annunciation of the birth of Isaac, Sarah takes the lead. She is named more often than her husband, for it is she who has suffered the humiliation of sterility and whom the angels of God come to visit (Gen 18:1–15).

A Liberating Laugh

At the time of the second announcement of the birth of a child, Sarah is not present. She who is at the center of the event is hidden at the entrance of the tent. Upon hearing the news, she begins to laugh to herself (Gen 18:12). Her husband had apparently not informed her of the first announcement (Gen 17:19). Consequently, she is at first surprised, and then because she is a woman, she makes gentle fun of seeing these men talk among themselves about motherhood.

This laugh of Sarah's actually has a much more profound significance. We readers, both men and women, know this psychological reaction well—the little nervous laugh that escapes from us when we learn after an agonizing wait that the weight of our fear has suddenly been lifted. Some cry, and others laugh. The latter is the case with Sarah. For her it is a liberating laugh. Her laugh is in fact connected with a long humiliation, with the moral suffering caused by her status as a sterile wife. It is not only a liberating laugh but also a laugh of joy, a laugh of faith. She thinks, "After I have grown old, and my husband is old, shall I have pleasure?" (Gen 18:12) If we compare her reaction to that of Zachariah who demands proof that his already old wife Elizabeth will really become pregnant (Luke 1:18), we see that there is not the least trace of doubt in Sarah's laugh. On the contrary, all the women of the Bible who have had to suffer the curse of sterility, when it is taken from them, have known, each in her own way, how to express joy and thanksgiving. Sarah laughs, and later Rachel will cry, "God has taken away my reproach" (Gen 30:23).

There is of course the dialogue between Abraham and the Lord (Gen 18:13–15) that seems to contradict our interpretation. However, if we set aside the fact that the biblical text is usually centered on men, viz., androcentric, and read it with Sarah's eyes, a woman's eyes, we believe that there is no contradiction. When Sarah denies having laughed, it is because she is afraid. She is afraid, not of God and God's promises, but rather of the curse attached to sterility. Years of suffering and being despised cannot be forgotten in an instant.

In this dialogue God is really addressing Abraham's wife. She is told in language she can understand that God is close to the brokenhearted, the humiliated, the rejected, which is who Sarah is in this patriarchal society where sterile women have no place. And when the Lord says to her, "Oh yes, you did laugh" (Gen 18:15), God is not reproaching her. With these words she is simply being told that God has understood her drama as a woman, that God participates in it in the divine fashion by making her fertile, for with God nothing is impossible.

Sarah's laugh is expressive of her whole story right up to the meeting at Mamre. It is the summation of all her stifled words, all her hidden tears. It is a marvelous laugh, which breaks out in liberating promises for her and for her people. Yes, truly God has given her reason to laugh (Gen 21:6).

From One Woman to Another

Even though Sarah could be seen as an image of conjugal fidelity, of virtue, of the Church even, for us today she is above all a woman. She is the first one in the Bible to be presented with all the facets of her personality and in the different stages of her life, a life which the Hebrew text tells us literally, lasted one hundred years and twenty years and seven years (Gen 23:1). This is a strange way of saying that "Sarah lived one hundred twenty-seven years," as the NRSV and other current versions of the Bible translate it. According to Rashi* the reason the word "years" is repeated after each number is that each number of years contains its own meaning. "At one hundred years she was like a twenty-year-old, still beautiful; at twenty years, she was like a seven-year-old, without sin."

Then at the time of the journey into Egypt, by herself she chooses to take responsibility for her husband's life. The long years of suffering without a child end with the birth of Isaac, but the difficulties with Hagar occur along with the ultimate test which will cause her death, the "binding" of her son. Since Isaac was not in fact "sacrificed" but only "bound" on the altar, we prefer the Jewish expression "binding" to designate what Christians usually call the "sacrifice of Isaac."

In each of these stages not only is Sarah revealed as a free and autonomous woman but also as what one could call an archetype, that is to say, the first exemplary figure in a new line. It is she who really opens the door for the other women of the Bible and, more immediately, for the other matriarchs. She is tightly connected to the spouses of the patriarchs, especially to Rebekah.

Indeed, it is Rebekah who will succeed Sarah and not Keturah, Abraham's new wife (Gen 25:1). To demonstrate better that there is a succession and continuity between the vocations of Sarah and Rebekah, the latter's birth is announced just before Sarah's death (Gen 22:23). And when Rebekah becomes Isaac's spouse, she fills the void left by Sarah's death, as though history could not go on without Sarah's presence: "Then Isaac brought her into his mother Sarah's tent. He took Rebekah, and she became his wife; and he loved her. So Isaac was comforted after his mother's death" (Gen 24:67). In this chain of events we have the beginning of a genealogy from woman to woman like the one from man to man, but with this important difference, that the matriarchs who are not linked by blood ties leave each other not a material inheritance (Gen 25:5) but a spiritual one.

The Midrash* that teaches us what one matriarch confides to another reads as follows:

> Throughout Sarah's life, a cloud hovered over her tent, but at her death this cloud disappeared. It returned when Rebekah arrived. Throughout Sarah's life, the gates were open wide, but at her death they were closed, and no one else was received. Hospitality, however, began again when Rebekah arrived. Throughout Sarah's life, there was a blessing in the bread dough, but at her death it disappeared. When Rebekah arrived, it returned. Throughout Sarah's life, a light was lit each Sabbath that burned till the next, but at her death this light was extinguished. However, this light shone again when Rebekah arrived. And when Isaac perceived that Rebekah walked in the steps of his mother, he made her come into his tent. His tent, thanks to Rebekah, became once again the tent of Sarah his mother.

This enumeration picks up all the elements that form the heart of Jewish daily life and also those of the divine presence in the midst of social life. That is why "before the Holy One, blessed be the Holy One, permitted Sarah's sun to set, the Holy One made Rebekah's sun rise."

At the moment Sarah disappears, the fulfillment of the promise is confided to another couple, Isaac and Rebekah. Abraham, who has several other children with his new wife, ends his life away from the adventure of the promise.

But God does not forget. God blesses him one more time "so that people do not say, 'Abraham has only benefited from the merits of his holy spouse.'" It would appear therefore that Sarah is really the central character in the story of Abraham, and the history of the promise continues through Isaac, Sarah's son. From this we can deduce that the sign of the promise is to be Sarah's son and not Abraham's, since Abraham has numerous other sons who are not taken into consideration (Gen 17:19–21).

Sarah the Prophet

Sarah's personality is too rich and complex to be defined, as has so often been done, simply by the three terms of sterility, laughter, and motherhood. Nothing human is foreign to her, and this fact is perhaps what makes her a divine presence. Throughout her life we find her turned toward God and toward others. Time after time she appears as both generous and possessive, patient and passionate, virtuous and yet jealous, agonized. She is also a prophet, a tool of God.

We recall that Sarah had dared to make (Gen 12) what we have called a "messianic choice" in putting her husband's good before her own. This biblical text is essential. It is like a prelude to all the successive themes of the history of God's people. It announces the exodus of Moses and the liberation from Egypt (Exod 7–15), all the elements of which are already present: the famine which draws them into exile in Egypt, the important role of Pharaoh, the plagues inflicted on Pharaoh's house, the liberation, and the return.

In Genesis 12 the central character of the liberation is Sarah. Her messianic choice places her beside Moses, or better yet, she presages him. We can even say that she is the "forerunner" of Joseph and Moses. This Egypt is both seductive and destructive, and she shows that salvation is possible.

The most important events in Sarah's life are always events connected with death. A table borrowed from Jean Vanel outlines three decisive moments: the descent into Egypt (Gen 12), the dismissal of Hagar (Gen 21), and the binding of Isaac (Gen 22). To visualize Sarah's role better, this table shows who or what is responsible in each event, who risks life, who dies, and finally who the savior is.

The decisive moments	Who/ what is responsible?	Who risks life?	Who dies?	Who saves?
Descent into Egypt	Famine	Abraham	—	Sarah
Dismissal of Hagar	Sarah	Hagar and Ishmael	—	God
Binding of Isaac	God	Isaac	Sarah	God

In each of these events Abraham is present, and he even plays an important role. He might always be front and center, but Sarah is the one who is making the decisions. In dangerous situations she is more combative, less fearful than her husband, and her decisions often turn out to be prophetic. Think about the dismissal of Hagar and Ishmael. Without the risk that Sarah dares to run for the mother and son, how would Hagar and Ishmael have been able to fulfill their vocation? Like God, Sarah puts the lives of others in danger, but she also saves them. Of all of them in the end, she is the only one to die. Indeed, the biblical story has the binding of Isaac followed by his mother's death (Gen 22–23). Rashi* comments on the succession of the two events thus: "Learning that her child has been bound on the altar, that he was ready to be immolated, that he was almost sacrificed, her soul left her, and she died."

Perhaps we can also establish a relation between this commentary by Rashi* and the fear which Sarah felt at the moment of the announcement of Isaac's birth (Gen 18:15). Might the prophet Sarah in the space of an instant have foreseen the binding of her son Isaac, the dreadful test that causes her death, and that marks forever the life of the second patriarch?

Sarah's laugh also seems to be prophetic. It is liberating laughter that announces the songs of other liberations—Miriam's on the banks of the Red Sea (Exod 15.20 21), Deborah's (Judges 5), Anna's (1 Sam 2:1-10), Judith's (Judith 16:1-17), and Mary's (Luke 1:46-55).

"Darkness is the black of Torah; light is the white of Torah."

2. HAGAR

It is scarcely possible to speak of Hagar without referring to Sarah, for Hagar's story overlaps the story of Sarah's loves and the drama of her sterility.

Sarah is the woman of two loves, her love for her husband and her love for her son. She does not understand unbiased love, as Abraham, always the mediator (Gen 13:7-12; 18:16-33), seems to do. Her love for her husband is not without impatience. When therefore, after a number of years of married life she observes that the divine promise is still not fulfilled, she decides to give Hagar, her Egyptian slave, to her husband.

Sumero-Babylonian law foresaw the possibility chosen by Sarah and would have made Hagar Abraham's "transitional spouse." The Sumerian code also outlines the consequences of this act. When the slave is pregnant, she does not have the right to pose as her mistress's rival. Hagar remains a slave, and her passing relations with Abraham have no other end than to give the possibility of fertility to the sterile couple.

The Daughter of Pharaoh

But who is Hagar the Egyptian? Perhaps she is one of the slaves that Pharaoh gave to Abraham as a gift (Gen 12:16). Rashi* tells us that "never had any slave or servant left Egypt free except Hagar." And he adds, "She was the daughter of Pharaoh. When he saw the miracles done for Sarai, he said, 'It would be better for my daughter to be a servant in such a house as this than mistress in another house.'"

The Islamic tradition also says that Hagar was Pharaoh's daughter. That tradition reports the event that makes her a servant in Abraham's house this way: "When Pharaoh wanted to take Sarah for himself, his hand was paralyzed. He then asked Sarah to invoke God in order to give him back the use of his hand. The scene transpired three times, and three times Sarah freed him. Knowing that he would not be able to have this woman, he sent for the man who had brought Sarah and ordered him to take her away and gave her Hagar as a servant . . . After this adventure, Sarah returned to her husband accompanied by Hagar. Sarah, sterile and too old to hope to give birth, delivered Hagar to Abraham; the servant gave birth to Ishmael."

In this episode where the future of the couple Sarah and Abraham is being played out, two women have a similar, but different, destiny. Both become woman-gifts: Sarai for Pharaoh and Hagar for Sarai. Nahmanides says in a commentary that when Sarai gives Hagar as a wife to Abraham, it is "with respect for the dignity of her husband." This causes us to think that Sarai might be remembering how she herself lived at the court of Pharaoh. When she raises her slave to the rank of spouse, she does so as an act of female solidarity. The solution at which she finally arrives is not pleasant for anyone, neither for Sarai who loves her husband, nor for Hagar who is still young. Also, as Abraham is already an old man, is this choice really at all a pleasant solution? Therefore, if it is possible for her to lighten, however little, her servant's fate, why would she not do so?

Hagar's joy when she knows she is pregnant is so great that she is remiss in her duties to her mistress. "Does not this child glorify the despised body of its Egyptian slave mother?" asks France Quéré. But Sarai takes offense at her servant's cheerfulness and feels neglected by her. Once again she suffers as a sterile wife, this time because of the life that is developing in Hagar, and so she breaks into a fit of jealousy. Sarai exercises the right that Sumero-Babylonian law gives her in asking her husband to choose (Gen 16:5–6).

Abraham, whose tendency is always to want to conciliate, and who knows the generosity of his wife, hands Hagar over to Sarai in cowardly fashion. Although the law was perfectly respected, Jewish tradition judges "Sarai guilty of having acted in that way and Abraham guilty of having tolerated it. Therefore, God sees Hagar's misery and gives her a son who became the ancestor of a race that was to treat the descendants of Abraham and Sarah with harshness."

The Flight into the Desert

In the face of all this, Hagar goes off into the desert. She flees in solitude just as Elijah later flees, also from a woman's jealousy, to take refuge in the desert (1 Kgs 19). In the solitude of the sand the sky comes closer. An angel of the Lord comes to meet her, and near a well he initiates a dialogue with her that foreshadows the conversation of Jesus with the Samaritan woman (John 4). Hagar can recount to him her wretchedness as a slave-wife and servant.

The angel then announces to her, in the way he will later do to Mary (Luke 1:26–38), that she will have a son who will be called Ishmael, which means "God hears." In this way God restores Hagar to her dignify as wife and mother and promises her numerous descendants (Gen 16:7–15).

After having seen God and having been seen by God, Hagar has the courage to return to Sarai. The biblical text tells us nothing of her life as a young mother, just as we do not know what becomes of her in the patriarchal family. This is a discreet silence that lets us imagine that her life was not always easy and harmonious.

Expulsion of the Servant and her Son

We meet Hagar again only at the time of the birth of Isaac. Ishmael at that time must have been about fourteen years old, and so he is almost an adult when the second drama between Sarah and her servant breaks out.

If Abraham is deeply attached to his first son, to the point of crying out at the announcement of the birth of a child with Sarah: "O that Ishmael might live in your sight!" (Gen 17:18) this is definitely not the case for his wife. Over the years, Ishmael had become his father's promised son. Now God is telling him that this is not to be the case, for it is with Isaac that he will make a covenant, not with Hagar's child (Gen 17:18-22).

As for Sarah, the biblical text is not forthcoming. We have to suppose that for fourteen years she was filled with contrary feelings, the joy of seeing Ishmael born, the knowledge that he was the child of her servant and not her own, and the ongoing reminder of her suffering as a sterile wife. She probably even asked herself if she was right to give her servant to her husband. She does not yet know that they are both called to a particular destiny. Therefore, when after so many years she becomes a mother in her turn and mother of the son of the covenant, this child is all that counts in her eyes.

The drama breaks out on what appears to be a futile pretext, but one which shows us the tension in which Sarah and Hagar live. Seeing Ishmael have fun during a feast that his father offers on the day of Isaac's weaning, Sarah asks her husband brusquely to send the mother and her son away (Gen 21:8–10). This time Abraham does not obey; he becomes angry, for Ishmael is his very dear son.

To give us a better idea of what has happened, let us examine the Islamic tradition. This tradition "imagines a sporting competition from which Ishmael leaves the winner. Abraham, in order to congratulate his eldest, had him sit on his knees as a sign of affection, while he placed Isaac at his side. Sarah conceived her jealousy from this event. To give her satisfaction, Abraham suggested that she take her revenge and humiliate Hagar by piercing her ears." Another narrative reports "that the two children squabbled and that it degenerated into a dispute between the two women. Sarah, in the name of the legitimacy of her status, demanded that Abraham banish Hagar. Abraham resigns himself to the task, but not without difficulty, and leads Hagar and Ishmael into a deserted place in that valley of Mecca of which the Quran speaks."

Jewish tradition says that "of all the tests that Abraham had to undergo, this dismissal was particularly sad for him" In fact it took no less than a divine intervention for the patriarch finally to accept bending himself to his wife's wish: "But God said to Abraham, 'Do not be distressed because of the boy and because of your slave woman; whatever Sarah says to you, do as she tells you, for it is through Isaac that offspring whall be named for you. As for the son of the slave woman, I will make a nation of him also, because he is your offspring" (Gen 21:12–13).

Hagar the Founder

Islamic tradition has this text:

> Abandoned, Hagar runs after her husband and master and challenges him, "To whom do you leave us?" But when Abraham vows to her that it is the command of Allah, she submits and becomes confident again. "If Allah has decreed it, we will not be abandoned."
>
> The water skin is quickly empty, and Hagar looks for water crying for help. She goes toward the nearest mountain, Safa Hill, north of the Mecca Valley. Hearing the roar of a lion, she fears for her son and runs to him. Again she hears a voice coming from the Marwa Hill, and she goes toward it. She thus becomes the first to complete the "pilgrimage" between the two hills of Safa and marwa, which has become a liturgy for Muslims.

> Hearing the voice of a man whom she cannot see, she begins to cry for help. "Hear me, God! Come to my aid, for I am perishing with my child." The angel Gabriel comes to her and leads her to the wells of Zamzam. The angel strikes the earth and a spring surges up. Seeing Hagar dig around the running water to prevent it from flowing away, Gabriel reassures her by confiding to her that this well will give water in abundance and that later pilgrims, guests of God, will quench their thirst her. He also predicts that the father and the child will one day come and build a sanctuary to the Lord on the same place."

This narrative from the Islamic tradition gives Hagar a founder's place; she is the originator of the pilgrimage to Mecca. Thanks to her, this place that was only an agony of solitude, a shadow of death, becomes a holy place where, right up to the present, pilgrims come to drink.

It is interesting to note that the Islamic tradition has the divine will intervening in the dismissal of Hagar and her son: "It is Allah's command." In the text of Genesis Sarah sends the mother sand child away for a peccadillo, and God offers no contradiction. On the contrary, God confirms her judgment and even asks Abraham to obey his wife, "Whatever Sarah says to you, do as she tells you" (Gen 21:12).

So that the divine promises are fulfilled completely, it seems that God once again wants to be reassured of the availability of all. Before renouncing Isaac, Abraham is asked to renounce Ishmael, and Hagar is asked to accept the risk of her son's life and even her own, for who can survive in the desert with only a bottle of water? Sarah also has to make the terrible decision to put two lives in danger so that the divine promises will be fulfilled. It is at such a price that both women will become mothers of great peoples (Gen 15:5; 16:10).

In the lives of Sarah and Hagar we find singular meaningful similarities. Their meeting takes place when both are objects of commerce. While both are being offered as woman-gifts, they solve a difficult problem in which two men are in danger—Abraham risks his life, and Pharaoh risks losing his reputation as a man.

Because of Sarah's sterility, these two daughters of a king become wives of Abraham. Hagar, the "transitional wife," is the first to know the joys of motherhood. Sarah has to wait to see God's promise accomplished. The two sons that are born in the house of the patriarch are both the firstborn of separate posterities. We might wish that the biblical text told us if the two women had any conversation about the promises relating to the births of their sons.

The Binding of Ishmael

The narrative of the departure of Hagar and Ishmael begins with the same words as that of the departure of Abraham and Isaac for Mount Moriah, "Abraham rose early in the morning" (Gen 21:14; 22:3). This suggests that we put the two texts side by side and speak of the "binding of Ishmael" as well. This way we can show the similarity and not use the word "sacrifice" which, as we have seen, does not reflect what happens—Isaac was only "bound" on the altar and not put to death—and which today, on another count, is too charged with history.

Hagar (Gen 21:10-20)	Abraham (Gen 22:1-17)
Hagar has to leave, sent away by Sarah. (10-13) Abraham arose early in the morning and took a skin of water, which he gave to Hagar. She left to wander in the desert of Beersheba. (14)	Abraham has to leave, put to the test by God. (1-2) Abraham arose early in the morning, took his son Isaac and wood for the sacrifice and left. (3) Abraham took the wood, loaded it on Isaac, and took the flint and the knife. They left together. (6) Abraham bound his son and put him on the altar. (9) He reached out to take the knife and sacrifice his son. (10)
She cast her son under some bushes. (15) She went aside to sit. She raised her voice and wept: "Do not let me look on the death of the child." (16) The angel of the Lord called to Hagar, "Do not be afraid, for God has heard the voice of the boy where he is. (17) Come, lift up the boy, and hold him fast with your hand." (18) God opened her eyes, and she saw a well of water, filled the skin, and gave the boy some to drink. (19)	The angel called to him from heaven, (11) "Do not lay your hand on the boy or do anything to him." (12)
God was with the boy as he grew up, lived in the desert, married (20) and God made of him a great nation. (18)	Abraham opened his eyes and beheld a ram caught by its horns. He got it to offer in sacrifice instead of his son. (13) "I will indeed bless you," God said, "and I will make your offspring numerous . . ." (17)

Putting these two narratives alongside each other, we cannot fail to be struck by the similarity of Hagar and Abraham's experiences. Both undergo a time of intense suffering before finally knowing God's mercy. These two narratives also show us that Abraham had to renounce a son two times.

In fact before obeying God's command and offering Isaac, Abraham first had to obey the voice of God, which asked him, by Sarah's intercession, to renounce his firstborn son Ishmael. And we know from the various traditions, which are unanimous on this point, how much the patriarch loved his elder son. God therefore asked of Abraham a double sacrifice.

This was the second time that Hagar had the experience of both solitude and the nearness of God. The one who had seen her near a well, the "well of Beer-lahai-roi" (Gen 16:13–14), now comes to open her eyes and show her the well and give her, as well as her son, a new hope of life. In opening her eyes, God shows her that while what she is experiencing may have been due to Sarah's jealousy, it is now the way that she must live in order to become the mother of a great people.

We should also note that in the two narratives Ishmael is presented as a little child or as a boy, according to the translations, whereas Isaac, fourteen years younger, is described as a young man. This patriarchalization of the biblical text is unfortunate insofar as it takes away all the drama of life from Ishmael's point of view. While the commentators often emphasize Isaac's courage as he clearly submits to being bound on the altar, we are not sensitized in the same way to Ishmael's and Hagar's situations. On the other hand, in presenting Ishmael as a little child, are we perhaps also being shown Sarah's cruelty as she alone decides to send the mother and her little son away? This discrepancy prevents us of course from truly comparing the two adventures in these passages.

Tradition, the traditions actually, always emphasize the binding of Isaac to the detriment of that of Ishmael. Islamic tradition has vacillated for a long time between Isaac and Ishmael as the child nearly sacrificed, and it has opted for Ishmael by reading his name in place of Isaac's.

By putting the two texts in parallel as we have done, this substitution would seem not to be necessary, for it is both sons that Abraham has had to renounce, first his firstborn Ishmael and then his younger son Isaac. To speak of the "binding" of Ishmael therefore does not seem too strong. Even if the image is not altogether adequate, it has the merit of stressing that Hagar's son, once the water is gone, was exposed to death in the same way that Isaac was on the altar. Perhaps he was exposed to an even more atrocious end.

Abraham's Love for his Eldest

The resemblance of both Ishmael's and Isaac's destinies is found even in their father's affection. In spite of the departure of Hagar and her son, Abraham did not stop loving his son, as Jewish tradition testifies. Rabbi Eliezar tells how

> Abraham went to visit his son Ishmael three years after his departure, and he ordered Sarah not to get down from the camel at Ishmael's tent. He arrived there in the middle of the day and found his daughter-in-law. To the question, "Where is Ishmael?" she answered that he had gone to gather dates in the desert with his mother. He said

to her, "Give me some water and bread, for I am tired after traveling in the desert." She answered, "I have neither water nor bread." Abraham said to her, "When Ishmael comes back, you will tell him that an old man came from Canaan who said that his threshold was in bad shape." When his wife gave him this message, Ishmael sent her away, and his mother had him marry another woman of her own family named Petouma. Three years later Abraham came back to see his son again. He was absent as before, but his wife gave his father something to eat and drink. Abraham prayed for his son and blessed the house. When Ishmael learned of this on his return, he knew that his father still loved him."

And Rashi* adds, referring to Genesis 22:3, "Ishmael then returned to his father's house at Beer-Sheba, and he accompanied his father at the time of the test, of the 'binding' of Isaac."

Islamic tradition has preserved a very similar narrative of the double visit of Abraham to Ishmael:

Abraham was seized with nostalgia for his elder son and asked Sarah's permission to visit him. He did it a first time, but he was not well received by the wife of the absent Ishmael. Abraham left his son a message, "Change the threshold of your house." Ishmael received the message, understood what his father meant, and divorced his wife. At his second visit the new daughter-in-law welcomed her father-in-law. Ishmael was out hunting, and Abraham had her tell him, "Keep the threshold of your house." Ishmael thereby learned of Abraham's promise to come back and founded a sanctuary in the place."

The unanimity of these texts testifies clearly to the affection that united father and firstborn.

Rivals and Sisters in Turn

It is not easy to define Hagar's place in the Abraham saga. The Bible does speak of her whenever an important event occurs in Sarah's life. Otherwise, Hagar is left in the shadow. Does this mean that the fulfillment of their vocations necessarily implied a separation? Did Sarah's peremptory character and status as legitimate wife prevent Hagar from finding her own place and from seeing a female solidarity develop between two women with such similar fates? It is really hard to answer these questions and to reconstruct the story of these two women from texts that give them both such small roles.

Like Sarah, Hagar gave birth to a people and to one of the great monotheistic religions. In the story of the covenant Hagar and Ishmael have specific roles too. We can wonder if Sarah would have given birth to Isaac if Ishmael had not been born first. In fact, modern psychology asserts the importance of adoption in cases of sterility. We know of families that, after the adoption of one or two children, have had the joy of procreation.

As for Hagar's son, in Sarah and Abraham's family he is the sign of God's absolute freedom. Although he was the elder and perhaps his father's favorite son, he was not the one to transmit Abraham's name to his posterity. Rather it was his younger brother who did that (Gen 21:12). His birth testifies to the fact that God blessed Sarah's deed in order to fulfill the promise. And while there is of course a difference between the two children, God is equally connected to both (Gen 21:20; Deut 21:15-17).

As the elder, Ishmael demonstrates the importance of human effort, but he also shows us its limits. Abraham and Sarah could very well have been contented with this son and have let their personal hope be extinguished. As we have said, Abraham almost renounced the idea of having a child by Sarah (Gen 17:17-19). But Isaac represents a temptation too, the temptation to passivity, and this is why two sons had to be born to Abraham and also why both had to be given back to God.

Rivals and sisters in turn, Sarah and Hagar needed each other. Sarah needed Hagar, as later Naomi did Ruth, in order to keep hope. Hagar needed Sarah's sad decision that sent her into the desert in order to fulfill her own destiny.

While the Bible does not speak of reconciliation between Sarah and Hagar, it does tell us that their two sons met to bury their father Abraham (Gen 25:9). It also tells us that after his mother's death Isaac lived in the Negev and of his own free will visited Beer-lahai-roi, the place where God visited Hagar and received the divine promise (Gen 24:62). Finally, Rashi* does not hesitate to identify with Hagar the last wife of Abraham, Keturah, because, as he says, from the time of her separation from the patriarch, Hagar remained chaste—in Hebrew "kashei," from the root "katar" from which Keturah is derived (Gen 25:1).

Hagar the Foreigner

Given as a gift of Pharaoh to transients who were fleeing famine, Hagar the Egyptian, although a foreigner in the land of Canaan and "transitional wife" in Abraham's family, is not just any old wife. Quite the opposite, in her is

fulfilled one of the divine wishes present in all Scripture
and to be sung about by Mary in her Magnificat: the
humble, the hungry, those who fear God have been lifted
high, and the arrogant of heart and mind has God routed
(Luke 1:52–53).

Hagar opens the door for all the foreign women cited
in the genealogy of Jesus: Tamar, Rahab, Ruth, Bathsheba.
These women played an important role in salvation history, just as Hagar played an indispensible role in the story
of the promise. Hagar presages even more the Canaanite
woman, the Samaritan, the prostitutes, the publicans, the
lepers, all those who in one way or another are despised,
unknown, rejected.

As a foreigner she also opens the door for Sarah, in
some way. When Sarah's turn comes, and she is raised
from her humiliation as a sterile wife to conceive a son,
she is only following in the path of the despised Hagar,
given as a slave and then as a concubine, and who found
her dignity as a wife and mother in the birth of Ishmael.

Hagar is not a minor biblical figure. For us women
she is the one who saw God after having been seen by God
(Gen 16:13–14). There are very few people indeed who
have seen God. There is Jacob at the ford of the Jabbok,
and the experience renders him infirm (Gen 32:22–32).
There is also Gideon, but afterward he lives in the fear of
death (Judg 6:22–23), just as Samson's parents do (Judg
13:22). After his vision Isaiah cries, "Woe is me! I am lost;
yet my eyes have seen the King, the Lord of hosts" (Isa
6:5).

In each of these instances there is great fear. Yet for
Hagar it is altogether different. Her vision of God is always
connected to a well, a spring. For her, God is not a devour-

ing fire, something to fear; for her, God is very precious, like cool water in the desert (Gen 16:7-14; 21:19).

Hagar is surprising as she is indignant at her mistress's remarks (Gen 16:5–6) and yet remains silent when Sarah sends her away (Gen 21:8–14). Not a word of hatred, nor a gesture of retaliation. Was there, at a level that our reason cannot attain, a deep relationship between these two women? Doubtless there is a secret between Sarah and Hagar, a secret that remains theirs and that one can only dimly perceive in the silences of the biblical text, and in their silences.

"Behold the darkness—it is the print of Torah, and the light—it is between the lines of Torah."

two

Rebekah's Fruitful Solitude

A FTER HIS MOTHER'S DEATH Isaac finds consolation in marrying Rebekah, the daughter of Bethuel
(Gen 24:67). Because of her, the divine presence once
again glowed in Isaac's tent. But before succeeding Sarah,
Rebekah also has to break with her background in order
to become the wife of the son of the covenant. As Rashi*
tells us, "She was the daughter of an infidel, the sister of an
infidel, the inhabitant of a country of infidels."

The second matriarch appears first in Genesis 24.
There we discover a young woman who is charming to the
eyes, generous, and of a free mind. She has not one moment of hesitation before she gives a drink to the stranger
Eliezer, Abraham's servant (Gen 24:18). Her simple and
perhaps natural gesture in the desert, where thirst is often
cruelly felt, is the gesture of hospitality that Eliezer chooses as a sign of recognition. By giving a stranger a drink of
water from her jug, Rebekah becomes the daughter-in-law
of Abraham.

A Spontaneous Love

The text lets us see in Rebekah's charming traits a woman who is spontaneous and full of initiative (Gen 24:19,28). Her whole behavior reveals a decisive character; she is a person who knows her own mind. When her mother and brother propose that she delay her departure somewhat, she decides with firmness to leave the family home: "I will go to my own master even if you do not wish it" (Rashi*). Rebekah seems to be a bit of a rebel. It appears too that she had discerned in the nobility and delicacy of Eliezer's acts a behavior quite different from that to which her family had accustomed her. She guesses that where he comes from they have other customs. She feels instinctively attracted by those other customs, and she understands that she will find in Isaac someone she could be close to.

The story of Rebekah is the story of a marriage in which the desire (*eros*) for possession and power is absent. The love between Isaac and Rebekah is the kind that knows how to move from the greeting of two strangers to the reciprocity of two who respect each other's autonomy.

The "yes" that characterizes Rebekah's life is not the fruit of the reasoning of a young woman about the advantages and disadvantages of the proposition she had just received. She is moved by Eliezer's behavior and responds with acts that are straightforward and engage her whole being. This is why when her family tries to hold her back she again acts decisively. The new reality that she has sensed draws her toward the unknown. Like Abraham and Sarah, Rebekah breaks with her background, and she crosses the Syrian desert to become the wife of Isaac, Abraham's heir (Gen 24:55–59).

Rebekah's "yes" has all the warmth and joy and enthusiasm of love, a love that melts into a single force that is both *eros* and *agape*, desire and tenderness. On the threshold of married life she understands that being a spouse consists of becoming compassionate, as well as feeling passion and consenting to it. This is why, even though it is at least in part an arranged marriage, Isaac can love Rebekah and be entirely consoled by her when he receives her as his wife (Gen 24:67).

Isaac recognizes in Rebekah someone who will not only be a wife and give him children, but more essentially someone who will be his other half, someone who will participate fully in the fulfillment of the covenant, someone who can succeed Sarah. A single act makes this young woman the second matriarch, and this act contains two of Abraham's characteristic traits, namely, an unhesitating "here I am" and a definite act of hospitality. So when Isaac's servant tells him how things have gone, he understands right away that Rebekah is of the same spiritual family as his parents.

Jacob the Favorite

Like her mother-in-law, Rebekah is sterile. Then came twenty years of patience, which must have been twenty years of testing, questioning, and praying. The biblical text, centered as it always is on the men in the patriarchal narratives, tells us that God heard Isaac's prayer and had pity on him (Gen 25:21). We must smile when we read these lines, for women are the ones for whom sterility is a drama.

Fortunately for the story of the covenant, this pity for Isaac turns into motherhood. Rebekah is pregnant, and "the children struggled together within her" (Gen 25:22).

The fight inside her made her fearful. So she decides to consult God, and here we see the Lord addressing her directly. The Lord gives to her, and to her alone, a very important revelation: "Two nations are in your womb, and two peoples born of you shall be divided; the one shall be stronger than the other, the elder shall serve the younger" (Gen. 25:23).

When this unusual pregnancy comes to term, Rebekah gives birth to twin boys. But are they really? This is very probably the question their mother had to ask herself when she saw them. Esau who emerged first was red, hairy, wild looking. Jacob came next, his hand grasping his brother's heel, and is presented by tradition as a sweet person, refined, given to study. He is the opposite of his brother who only loves to hunt (Gen 25:24–27).

Isaac, the most settled of the patriarchs and yet a great lover of game, shows favoritism to Esau. On the other hand, Rebekah, who carries a divine secret, favors Jacob. Besides, "Who would blame her for preferring a man to a bear?" France Quéré asks. Moreover, if Isaac's choice is hardly surprising, the entrenched and peremptory behavior of his wife does pose some questions.

Why does Rebekah reject Esau? His physical appearance, less comely than that of his brother, is not a sufficient reason for a woman who, as we have seen, knows the compassionate side of love. Perhaps we must understand this rejection as the expression of yet another inner struggle that Rebekah had to undergo. This debate is already present in her from the moment of her pregnancy and tells her that irrational forces are lining up against each other in the two worlds symbolized by her two sons. These might well be the two worlds represented by her own family of origin and by the family of Isaac, heir of the promise.

By preferring Jacob, Rebekah reaffirms her choice in life, which was to fulfill the mysterious design of God. Fidelity to this choice will not be without suffering, and that fidelity draws Rebekah into a solitude that will be difficult at crucial moments of her life. Alone she has to act in defiance of her husband. Alone she will decide to send Jacob away in order to remove him from Esau's violent behavior.

A Decisive Action

Esau's life plunges his parents into sadness. Without regard for the customs of his family, he follows the leanings of his nature and chooses his wives from among the Hittites (Gen 27:1–5). Not only must such behavior have rendered family life difficult, but also it certainly made Rebekah think as she recalled God's word: "The elder shall serve the younger" (Gen 25:23). Even though she does not yet see how that word will come to pass, she remains attentive all the same. It is certainly not by chance that Rebekah hears the conversation between her husband and Esau (Gen 27:1–5). Like Sarah, perhaps she kept herself hidden in an obscure corner of the tent. At the very moment when she understands that Isaac is on the verge of handing down his blessing to Esau, her decision is made. She must intervene, because for the promise to be fulfilled, she must prevent her husband from making a mistake. If he has not perceived who Esau is, then the responsibility falls to her to make God's plan come to pass however she can.

She immediately outlines a plan for Jacob to follow. Here again we see the spontaneous and decisive behavior of the young woman who received Eliezer. When Rebekah perceives what is to transpire, nothing stops her. As resolutely as she acted before she left her people, so now she decides to mislead her husband. And she does it authoritatively as for the second time she asks Jacob to listen to her, that is, to obey her (Gen 27:8–13).

Rebekah is entirely resolved on her action, and this decision reminds us of Sarah expelling Hagar and her son. She takes on herself all the risks that her mother-in-law did. Alone she accepts the divine promise as she takes her bearings in order to fulfill it: "Two peoples born of you shall be divided; the one shall be stronger than the other, the elder shall serve the younger" (Gen 25:23).

Upon his mother's responsibility and advice, Jacob usurps the blessing promised to Esau. Although he simply executed his mother's plan, it is nonetheless against him that Esau unleashes his violence. Here we see for the third time Rebekah asking her son to obey her and flee the murderous anger of his brother (Gen 27:43). Beforehand she arranges for Isaac to bless his son's departure for Paddan aram where his uncle lived so that the promise might be fulfilled (Gen 28:1–5).

A Costly Decision

After this rush of events, all that is left is for Rebekah to pay the price of her decisions. So that the promise might be fulfilled, she loses both her sons. Her actions are motivated by a greater good than her desires as a mother. That, however, does not prevent her from finding herself deprived of her children. Everything in the lives of the matriarchs as well as the patriarchs centers on the divine promise.

It is likewise because of this promise that the biblical text speaks with such emotion about Jacob and inspires our dislike of Esau, who is after all the victim of this plot. As we have noted, because Isaac was the son of the covenant, the process was the same as for Hagar and Ishmael, the victims of Sarah's anger.

It is absolutely necessary that the promises of God be fulfilled, and Rebekah tries her best to avoid the fatal consequences of hatred and violence unleashed by her decisions. As she sends Jacob to his uncle Laban and accepts the suffering occasioned by this separation, she is pushed by a twofold fear. She fears seeing Esau become his brother's murderer, and she fears too that the promise would remain unfulfilled with Jacob dead (Gen 27:41–45).

Her decisions are motivated not only by fear, but also by love. Rebekah felt that in her elder son, as violent as he seems, the fire of brotherly love has not been entirely extinguished. She counts on the work of time to appease his anger. The astonishing encounter between the two brothers years later will prove her entirely right. The experience of life shaped Jacob and Esau as they grew older. Little by little, suffering found its rightful place and became the means of communion instead of division. This theme occurs as well when the prodigal son meets his father (Luke 15:20).

Jacob, dreading to meet his brother whom he knows he has wounded to the depths of his being, prepares a princely welcome. The biblical text needs twenty verses to describe these preparations. This shows us the importance he attaches to the reconciliation (Gen 32:2–22). Esau, like the father in the later parable, runs to meet his brother and takes him in his arms, and the text says, "They wept" (Gen 33:4). Esau's tears signify a welcome and unconditional pardon as well as the astonishment of newly found brotherly love. In the mutual respect two people have when they truly recognize each other, the free nature of love can finally be shown. It is perfectly possible to see in the middle of the brothers' embrace the presence of their mother Rebekah.

The plan Rebekah invented to fulfill the promise is not necessarily an exemplary one. In deceiving her husband, in frustrating Esau's promised blessing, she plunged her children into a violent situation for which she knew herself to be responsible. She played a role that is certainly not to her honor, but one for which she assumes complete responsibility. She is not content simply to say to herself, "Even in my womb the two boys were fighting . . ." Instead, she looks for ways that will limit any damage.

One of these ways is to remain alone and send each of her sons to his own destiny, a choice that arises from a mystical vision. She dares to believe in the possibility of reconciliation. Likewise, she has the wisdom to leave her children in complete freedom. If they wish, they will find a path to reconciliation by themselves. In order to act in this way, she had to have great confidence and faith along with the certainty that if she were responsible for her acts right to the end, God will prove to be no less faithful.

Scripture devotes only a few pages to Isaac and Rebekah as a couple, and we know nothing more of the life of the second matriarch from the time when, daring to suggest a nearly unthinkable plot of which she is prepared to take all the consequences, she assures the survival of the people of God by giving her own destiny free play.

We do not even know if the grandmother of the twelve tribes of Israel had the joy of playing with her grandchildren.

three

Rachel and Leah

Rivals but also Allies

STRENGTHENED BY THE PATERNAL blessing (Gen 27:27–29; 28:1–4) and by the assurance of divine protection (Gen 28:10–22), Jacob went off without a worry to his uncle Laban's house to look for a wife.

The Well of Meeting

It is near a well in the land of his ancestors that Jacob meets the shepherd Rachel (Gen 29:1–12.). The place is important, for as we recall it was also near a well that Isaac's marriage was decided (Gen 24:15–27), and it will also be near a well later that Moses' marriage will be concluded (Exod 2:15–22).

In the Bible we frequently see a well and all the acts that transpire at it associated with a woman. Besides the examples that we just gave, we also find Miriam's well. According to tradition it gave water for forty years to the Hebrew people in the desert. Thanks to Miriam it did not dry up (Exod 15:22–25; Num 20:1–8). In the Second

Testament at Cana during a marriage Mary intervenes with Jesus, for the guests have no more wine. Then the water drawn into jars is changed into wine (John 2). And it is likewise near a well, Jacob's well at that, where Jesus met the Samaritan woman (John 4).

The well and the water associated with it are the source of life and joy, and often the source of understanding as well. The Hebrew word "beer" that means "well" can also mean "understanding" or "explanation." Hence, the well becomes a place of revelation.

In a collection of rabbinical commentaries edited in Palestine in the fifth and sixth centuries, in the Rabbah Midrash,* Rabbi Yo'hanan explains the meeting of Rachel and Jacob (Gen 29:1–8) in this way: "The well is Sinai. The three flocks: the priests, the Levites, Israel. From this well they drew up the Ten Commandments. The great rock is the Presence. All the flocks were alike, for if one Hebrew was missing, Israel would not have received the Torah. They removed the rock to hear the Voice."

Not just water, which is indispensable for desert nomads, nor even a metaphor, the well is the witness of numerous encounters and existential revelations that transform the lives of those who find themselves there (Gen 24:10–27; 29:1–10; Exod 2:15–22; John 4:1–42). Of all the wells of which Scripture speaks, Jacob's well is certainly the most familiar to us. The place of the meeting of the patriarch and the shepherd, it is also the location of the conversation between the Samaritan woman and Jesus in the course of which it is revealed that "salvation is from the Jews" (John 4:22). We can consider the passage from John as a midrash* on Genesis 29. In fact Jacob, who has become Israel, is the father of the twelve tribes.

Moreover, it is to Israel that God entrusted the Torah*
with its mission to quench the thirst of the nations. The
text of Genesis (Gen. 29:8), as does the commentary of
Rabbi Yo'hanan, makes it clear that "all the flocks must be
gathered together."

Jesus, who is also the son of Jacob, received the
specifically Jewish calling to provide water for and bring
fruitfulness to all human deserts. This is why he teaches
the Samaritan woman—that is, all the nations—that salvation is from the Jews. He shows us through this woman
how to "remove the stone in order to hear the voice," how
to dip into the deep well of revelation without a bucket for
"water gushing up to eternal life" (John 4:14).

At the well of Sinai Israel received a special revelation
that made it a well for all the nations. In the Samaritan
desert at Jacob's well, Jesus the Jew brings a universal revelation to a foreign woman (John 4:23). Do we not have
here the two sides of a single calling: to give something to
drink to all women and men who are thirsty for the truth?

We must add to this what the Muslim tradition has
taught us about Hagar's wandering in the desert. In order
to save the mother and her son, God's angel Gabriel causes
a well to spring up in the desert that becomes a place of
pilgrimage where guests of God, as we noted above, will
always find something to quench their thirst.

We learn from the biblical text that all Israel must as-
semble three times a year at Jerusalem to meet God there,
to draw from the living well (Lev 23:1–8; Deut 16). Today
Jews, Christians, and Muslims have some idea, in more
or less conscious fashion, that work for more justice and
peace in the world cannot be done without an existential
link to Jerusalem, the "City of Peace". Therefore, we can-

not resist paraphrasing the text of Yo'hanan cited above:
The well is Jerusalem. The three flocks: Jews, Christians,
Muslims. From this well we must fetch love, compassion,
respect for neighbors and all others. The great rock: the
Spirit of God. All the faiths gather here, for if one is missing, humanity cannot receive the revelation of liberating
love. Together they remove the rock so that all may hear
the Voice.

The well where the shepherd Rachel and the exile
Jacob meet teaches us therefore that to survive we must
unite our efforts and come together to roll away the rock
and water the parched earth with justice and peace. And
that is possible only if we let ourselves be led by the Spirit
of God.

Occupation: Shepherd

Rachel is the only one of the matriarchs to have an occupation. She is a shepherd, as Moses' wife Zipporah was.
Jacob himself will adopt her occupation because he loves
her (Gen 29:18). From this line in the text the rabbis drew
several conclusions.

If Rachel is sent to the well with the sheep, it is because she does not yet have any brothers. Ordinarily this
work is confided to a man. Sons will not be given to Laban
until after Jacob's arrival (Gen 30:27; 31:1). Laban could
well have sent his eldest daughter. He did not do so because Leah, the eldest, ran a greater risk than her younger
sister. Whence the conclusion of the rabbis: Rachel had
not yet entered puberty, whereas Leah had. That explains
why Jacob had to wait such a long time before being able
to marry Rachel. And if a young woman had to guard the

sheep, that fact tells us that Laban is poor. At the time of Jacob's coming, his future father-in-law possesses only one little flock (Gen 30:30).

Rachel is therefore a very young shepherd, but one who seems to enjoy a special protection. In fact if we compare her meeting with Jacob to Moses' coming upon the daughters of Jethro, the difference is striking. Rachel, although young and alone, is not upset like the seven daughters of Jethro who are chased from the well by the shepherds (Exod 2:16–17). Besides, a girl alone was hardly ever respected, as the story of the rape of Dinah, Leah's daughter, proves (Gen 34).

It is likewise striking, as Abécassis emphasizes, that in this chapter, which is all about flocks, the only time that the word "shepherd" is used it is in the feminine to indicate that it refers to Rachel. There must also have been something special about her person, for as soon as Jacob sees her, he, whom tradition freely presents as weak, becomes strong enough to roll away by himself the stone that shepherds usually do not move without help (Gen 29:8–10).

Meeting Rachel therefore transforms Jacob. He begins to become who he already was but did not know it. Love lets him discover the strength that was dormant in him. Rachel reveals his passion, but also his tears. The encounter with the other, with the one who is our true counterpart, reveals our true self. That is why to the end of his life Jacob preferred Rachel to Leah.

Jacob's Tears

In Jewish symbolism, Rachel represents the Mother of Israel in mournful waiting for the return of the exiles (Jer 31:15). This is because from their first meeting Rachel and Jacob shed tears together (Gen 29:11). Such a determining and overwhelming meeting can truly provoke tears, tears of joy, for Jacob found the one who will be his counterpart, the one with whom he will share life fully. They are also tears of sadness, for Jacob is in exile. They have barely discovered each other when already they share the sorrow of exile. These prophetic tears announce Rachel's end, her grave by the side of a road, and not at Machpelah with the other matriarchs. Exiled from the family home, she waits, tradition tells us, until the last Jew returns to the Holy Land to rejoin her husband in the grotto of Machpelah.

These are tears of joy and tears of suffering, but also tears of hope in waiting for another return. Is not Rachel's arrival at the well the announcement to Jacob that a return is possible (Gen 27:45; 28:2)? But while waiting, they must work; this is why Jacob rolls away the rock and waters the flock.

Another interpretation of Jacob's tears is proposed by the Midrash.* Jacob wept because he heard it rumored that he, a foreigner, was introducing indecent customs into the land. He was bold enough to kiss Rachel, and to do it in public. Other rabbis suggest a more romantic and poetic interpretation. Jacob arrives in Rachel's land empty handed. He has nothing more to offer her than himself, his tears and his kisses (Gen 29:11; cf. Gen 24:22).

A Nonconformist Love

Explaining to us that Jacob's tears are caused by malevo-
lent comments, the Midrash* lets us imagine that Jacob
does not behave according to established norms. This is
because Jacob is a nonconformist. Love in the Bible takes
on a new face with Jacob. Only after their marriage is it a
question of love between Isaac and Rebekah (Gen 24:67).
With Jacob and Rachel it is the opposite. Love precedes
marriage. In addition, love dictates Jacob's choice. This
is a novelty compared with the arranged marriage of his
parents (Gen 24).

Jacob chooses his wife himself and freely offers seven
years of work before marrying her. Besides, he chooses the
younger, the one who the Midrash* says is not yet mar-
riageable. It was perhaps the case that Rachel's personality
was so strong and outgoing that Jacob could discern in
this very young woman the wife that she would become.

Whereas Esau had actually chosen a bigamous marriage (Gen 26:34), Jacob certainly did not foresee that his
own behavior would set in motion a stratagem on the part
of his father-in-law that would oblige him to become a
bigamous patriarch. When he does not refuse to give his
younger daughter in marriage, Laban also does not renounce the custom that says the older should marry first.
So it is that after offering seven years of labor for his beloved Rachel, Jacob, deceived by Laban, is obliged to accept
two wives. If he did not succeed in breaking the custom,
this arrangement does however bring along a variation on
the theme of sterility which recurs like a refrain in each
of the patriarchal and matriarchal generations: only the

beloved wife is sterile, and, forsaken by her husband, Leah is the one who has God's favor (Gen 29:28–31).

The Two Sisters

We can well wonder why in the story of Rachel and Leah the Bible, which so often upsets the usual order of nature and favors the younger, wants to respect the right of the elder here. Perhaps it had to be so before Jacob met his brother; he also had to experience the kind of deceit that totally reorients a life. It is very true that we only really understand an experience insofar as we know it personally.

The book of Zohar* tells us that Leah, the oldest daughter of Laban, was promised to Esau, the older son of Isaac. When she learns of Esau's behavior, Leah sheds many tears and prays that this marriage with a man of violence not take place. She beseeches God and waits for God's mercy to be greater than God's justice. By prayer essentially, Leah wants to change the course of her destiny. Although the Bible is entirely silent on this score and transmits in veiled terms only the mention of her delicate eyes, sad from so many tears, her revolt is no less radical (Gen 29:17). Leah refuses to be bound to a man like Esau and so testifies to her hope and her own choice for life.

Discreetly but with power, by her tears and prayer and without seeking to dominate or convince her sister, Leah prevents the forces of evil from overwhelming her. How then are we to understand the rest of the story? How can we explain why Leah accepts active participation in her father's trickery to take Rachel's place with Jacob? How should we interpret this seemingly egotistical and disloyal behavior?

The text is succinct and shows us Laban as the instigator of this trick (Gen 29:23–25). But could he act without the complicity of his two daughters? The Talmud* answers in the negative as it asserts the fact that the two lovers, Rachel and Jacob, foreseeing Laban's trick, decide on signals between them. Therefore on the wedding night Rachel, seeing "that Leah was going to be put in her place says to herself, 'For the moment my sister is going to be humiliated,' and she gives Leah the signs Jacob had devised for her."

The compassionate generosity of Rachel who lets her sister take her place arises from the behavior of the righteous, of those women and men who hold the world up by their radical choice of the good, that is, of life, and who give it flesh by gestures of free love where the good of the other is always placed ahead of their own. The compassion of Rachel who goes so far as to take on herself the unhappiness and sufferings of her sister recalls the gesture of Sarai assuming the agony of her husband (Gen 12:12–13). She also chooses the way of the Suffering Servant, daring to make a messianic choice that will affect her whole future. She is truly the lamb—that's what the name Rachel means after all—the lamb of which Isaiah speaks that is dumb before its shearers (Isa 53:7).

Jacob is so preoccupied with his love for Rachel that he does not see Leah's distress. When Rachel imposes on him the bodily presence of the one who is suffering the most, she is trying to open her husband's heart to the sufferings of others. Fully sharing with him the suffering that her act entails, she puts the two of them into a story that unravels so fast that it will leave them behind.

But Jacob remains faithful to his heart's first choice. Not only does he disdain Leah, but in serving Laban seven years for Rachel, he shows Leah that she is really nothing to him.

Love and Motherhood

We need only glance over the book of Genesis in cursory fashion to realize the importance of fertility in the patri-archal family. It is very often at the heart of the blessings, and usually it is to the man to whom it is given. That is the case in the fertility of Abraham (Gen 12:2; 15:5; 17:2,5–8; only Gen 16:10 mentions Hagar's, and Isa 51:2 Sarah's), the fertility of Ishmael (Gen 17:20–21), that of Isaac (Gen 26:4,24), that of Jacob (Gen 27:27; 28:3; 35:11; 48:4), that of Joseph (Gen 41:52; 49:22,25), and that of his sons (Gen 48:15–16).

All these blessings are related to the blessing God pronounced on the first couple Adam and Eve (Gen 1:28). In a patriarchal society to give birth to children in order to assure the continuation of the human race and the fam-ily is viewed as a sign of privilege. In this way the couple accomplishes what God expects of them, and fertility per-mits the man to hold his head high among his neighbors.

We keep meeting this from one end of the Bible to the other (cf. for example 1 Sam 1:2–10 and Luke 1:13–25), so true is it that the tendency to relate everything to the male occurs throughout. However when we read Scripture without this androcentric prejudice, we maintain, with Eliane Amado Lévy-Valensi, that "what is specific to the human couple is not based on the command to 'be fruit-ful and multiply'—that command was first given to the animals; neither is it reproductive or sexual—rather, it is dialogical."

It is truly in dialogue where man and woman are face to face as equal partners that history can be built on all levels, not simply on the level of procreation. The responsibility of men and women in history is infinitely greater and more complex. It is not simply through motherhood that women accomplish God's will. That is a distortion of God's will, one that permits men to have full authority and power over their wives. The plan of God, who created woman as a counterpart of man, is not to be found in an arrangement like that because it is in companionship that they pursue their work (Gen 2:22–24).

In the stories of the matriarchs all are sterile except Leah, and all except Rebekah give their servant to their husband in order to have a child. To understand this action, we must review a custom of the time and remind ourselves of "the obligation to give back gifts and presents that one has received under pain of losing face and freedom. The woman who does not give a child to her husband finds herself the debtor here. She is incapable of playing her role in the subtle but necessary game of exchange" (Gaston Wagner). She is therefore obliged to have recourse to a servant whose children will be recognized and adopted.

In Jacob's household Rachel and Leah are doubtless not treated equally in the matter of the frequency of sexual relations. Jacob prefers Rachel, the sterile one, and he neglects Leah who has already given him four sons. We find yet once more Jacob's nonconformity with respect to the customs of his time. The graciousness of his love for Rachel corresponds to God's plan for man and woman.

The fulfillment of that plan is not procreation to assure the continuity of the clan, but simply the desire to be together in the way they foresaw from the time of their meeting at the well. Thus Jacob's nonconformity conforms entirely to the will of God. While he served two times seven years for Rachel, he expects nothing from it in return except her love and presence to fulfill the divine promise. Moreover Rachel, a prisoner of the customs of the time, saw her sterility as God's judgment which will be definitively erased only by the birth of Joseph, her own child (Gen 30:23).

Leah, on the other hand, believes that she will finally be able to win her husband's love by giving him children. The names of her first four sons reveal the constancy of her desire to be loved (Gen 29:31–35). Jacob remains deaf to this language of childbearing however. In the story of Abraham and Hagar we saw faint outlines of the idea that procreation is not the way that defines the couple. What makes the marriage of Abraham and Sarah a union is the life of dialogue that exists between them, and to that life Sarah's sterility could be no obstacle.

This is what happens with Jacob. Love in the biblical sense is not a function, or simply a function, of procreation, of childbearing. Even if the text does not say so, Leah intuits that childbearing which is not an expression of shared love cannot do anything to give birth to a feeling which does not exist, or only barely exists in Jacob. Their common life seems to consist only in constraints (Gen 30:9,16). This prevents Jacob from discovering the secret of Leah's life. He does not understand that, constrained by patriarchal society to have children in order to be loved, she was waiting for him to awaken in her all the powers of her female being. In Leah he sees only the mother who gives birth, and she sees no more in Jacob than the father of her children.

Rachel's Jealousy

In spite of her love for her husband Rachel suffers from not having a child. The discredit that surrounds a sterile woman weighs heavily on her. Therefore, in order to combat this feeling of inferiority, she uses the same stratagem as Sarah. Pushed by jealousy, the text tells us (Gen 30:1) she too gives her servant to Jacob. Perhaps we are encountering a theme here, which since Cain and Abel, comes up in each generation. Certainly Rachel also wants "to have" children by Jacob, but she wants as much and maybe more "to give" children to Jacob. Her gesture is evidence of her feeling of jealousy, and it also signifies that she intends to participate actively in the building up of the family. In this sense, her jealousy is not just a negative feeling; it is also the expression of a creative desire.

Rachel expresses her feeling in words of great dramatic intensity: "Give me children, or I shall die!" (Gen 30:1). These words bother Jacob. The master of life is God, and he is not God (Gen 30:2). Does he not already have four children by Leah? The problem is not his. It concerns God and Rachel. Jacob declines all responsibility. He does not understand that his wife has an interior life and so is sadly frustrated in not having a part in building up the family.

Jacob's reaction of course still carries the mark of the rancor caused by the trickery and ridicule of his wedding night (Gen 29:22–30). The wound is not entirely healed, and he holds it against Rachel for being associated with this deceit. In spite of appearances, Jacob is not a simple person. He is not just the naïve lover who spontaneously offers years of his life to obtain the one he loves. He is also the one who, with his mother's help, tricked his own father and wounded his brother deeply. And at Laban's house he is not found lacking in devious means to get himself a flock of his own (Gen 30:36–43).

Rachel's gesture in giving her servant stops the exchange of words between the two spouses. That exchange is replaced by a sad and silent dialogue of love, in which Rachel and Jacob, each in turn, offer their suffering. The silence is in fact like a thick coat that envelopes and hides the dramatic aspect of this situation. Bilhah the servant also submits to this law of silence. Hidden in the shadow of her mistress, she has no right to say a word when Rachel gives her body away. Later at the time of choosing a name for her children, no one asks for her opinion. Rachel alone decides everything, invoking for her purpose God's justice (Gen 30:6). But Jewish tradition teaches that it is imprudent to trust in justice alone without including mercy, and this is why Rachel died prematurely at the birth of Benjamin (Gen 35:16–21).

Thanks to the custom of having children by giving a servant to one's husband, Rachel now has two sons. But her heart is not quiet. She remains marked by the thought that her sterility is a sign of God's judgment. Is this not what Jacob told her (Gen 30:2)? Therefore, when she cries out, "With mighty wrestlings I have wrestled with my sister, and have prevailed" (Gen 30:8), she expresses more her inner struggle than any victory.

In order to give children to Jacob and have a part in building the family, did she not have to give him Leah and

then her servant Bilhah? Was she right to do this? In spite
of these winding paths she is still a sterile woman. In this
cry, as in Sarah's laugh, we measure all the suffering that
sterility entails as well as the repressive power of tradition. Is one not alive in proportion to how one reproduces
through one's own "seed" (Gen 1:11)?

Both Rachel and her sister are in an inextricable situation. They see themselves constrained by every expedient
(Gen 30:9–13) to relate to the demands of a culture that
can envisage the existence of a woman only through her
childbearing.

Mandrakes

The episode of the mandrakes (Gen 30:14–21), those mandrakes that "give forth fragrance, and . . . choice fruits"
(Song 7:13), makes the drama that Jacob and his two wives
live concrete: Rachel's sterility, Leah's thirst for love, and,
in the middle, Jacob who becomes the victim of his two
wives in their race to motherhood. If it were not a question of very real suffering here, the scene would be comic.

One day Reuben brings to his mother Leah some
mandrakes, reputed at the time to have powers of fertility for women and aphrodisiacal powers for men. Rachel,
who had desired for such a long time to become a mother,
besought Leah to share them with her. Leah protests, "Is
it a small matter that you have taken away my husband?
Would you take away my son's mandrakes also?" Rachel
suggests a compromise however: "Then he may lie with
you tonight for your son's mandrakes." Sure of obtaining
some mandrakes for herself, she believes she will be able
to become fertile in her turn. When Jacob comes home

from work at the end of the day, the agreement between the two sisters has just been concluded. The biblical narrative tells us nothing of his reaction when it has Leah say to him, "You must come to me; for I have hired you with my son's mandrakes." What kind of a man would accept such a deal without saying a word? On the other hand, what is there to say when one suddenly understands the silent message of suffering?

Having grasped the shape of the situation, Jacob accepts the fact that once more Leah will take the place of Rachel, who thereby hopes to have the occasion of giving birth herself. While this substitution can be compared with his wedding night, it is also radically different from it. This time no one is duped. Jealousy cedes to solidarity, which emphasizes the tenderness that unites the two sisters. Jacob finally seems to penetrate the secret of his two wives. In this personal drama, in which they all have parts, each character finds some sort of transformation.

God even remembers Rachel and makes her fertile. The inner conflict is over. Rachel was not wrong in giving Leah, and then Bilhah, to Jacob. Her messianic choices bear fruit in a life that she calls Joseph. This child is now the sure sign that throughout those terrible years God had not forgotten her. For Rachel her son is the actualization of God's faithfulness. Joseph is divine tenderness made flesh (Gen 30:22–24).

A Departure Full of Risks

After the birth of Joseph, Jacob decides to leave Laban and return to his own country. But this termination of his exile looks like flight. Rather than have to confront the jealousy of Laban's family, and perhaps violence as before (Gen 27:41–43), he leaves. Before leaving however, he has another important conversation with his wives. He doesn't act like Abraham who, when he leaves, takes his wife and nephew along without consulting them. At the moment of leaving Harran to go home, Jacob reveals his intention and asks Rachel and Leah if they want to follow him. In doing so, he places before them the decisive choice with which all the matriarchs were acquainted: break with the past and leave home in order to form a new family (Gen 31:4–13).

Rachel and Leah's response is surprisingly clear and dignified. Treated like objects of commerce in their father's house, they evaluate their situation clearly and in complete freedom they choose Jacob's way of life. This is why they say to him, "Now then do whatever God has said to you" (Gen 31:14–16).

Before leaving her family however, Rachel takes advantage of her father's absence to carry off his teraphim, his household gods (Gen 31:19). We might well ask why Rachel commits this theft when she has decided to break not only with her family but also with their religion. Was it that she feared the power of Laban and his idols?

The Midrash* tells us that it is out of love that she did it, saying, "How is that? I am going away, and I would leave this old man to his errors?" So God comes to visit Laban in a dream, but he remains deaf to the divine counsel: "Take heed that you say not a word to Jacob, either good or bad" (Gen 31:24). One dares not imagine what would have happened if Rachel's very feminine ruse to distract her father's suspicions had failed (Gen 31:32,35).

Fortunately Laban finds nothing. And Jacob, entirely ignorant of Rachel's theft, takes advantage of the occasion furnished by his wife to tell his father-in-law everything he has in his heart. All the bitterness of the exploited foreigner comes out in his words, "God saw my affliction, and the labor of my hands, and rebuked you last night" (Gen 31:42). His sterile wife's sobs (Gen 30:22–26) are now echoed in the tears of the oppressed and exploited husband. God has decided to put an end to all these years of accumulated suffering. God has decided in favor of Laban's daughters and Jacob.

We will never know if Rachel was right to steal her father's household gods, but her boldness permitted Jacob to express the suffering that was in him. Also it gave her father the opportunity to conclude a treaty and to show his two daughters some tenderness (Gen 32:1).

Reconciliation

When Jacob returns to his own country and meets his brother, it is as though Rebekah were mysteriously present. In letting her younger son leave, had she not believed in a reconciliation between the twins (Gen 27:44–45)? Jacob's return cannot occur without a preliminary meeting with Esau. Jacob must finally confront the question of the rivalry between them. But before this decisive meeting angels come to comfort him (Gen. 32:1–2), for Jacob is afraid of his brother and fears for his wives, his children, and his property (Gen 32:12). So he makes the whole family cross the ford of Jabbok while he stays behind.

He remains alone in order to come to terms with this inner turmoil. This narrative (Gen 32:23–33), one of the most beautiful and best known in the Bible, describes a combat between doubt and confidence, between fear and courage, between what is of God and what is against God. This combat symbolizes how it is entirely possible for opposites to be reconciled. At dawn Jacob, having become Israel, is a new person through this reconciliation, but he is also a person who will remain marked in the flesh by the experience of this night at the ford of Jabbok till the day he dies. Elie Wiesel says that "Jacob emerges victorious from the fight, but this victory, a pure victory because it is without death and without humiliation, suggests nothing about the defeat of the adversary."

Therefore, after these hours of wrestling Jacob can go freely to meet his brother and thus realize Rebekah's hope and restore the broken bonds of brotherhood. In spite of appearances, Rebekah had judged the heart of her two sons well. Their meeting takes place not only in an atmosphere of brotherly affection but also of profound respect for each other's destiny (Gen 33:12–17).

The Ultimate Test

For Jacob and his family the return is staked out by emotions and tests. After the meeting with Esau comes the rape of Leah's daughter Dinah, followed by Simeon and Levi's bloody vengeance (Gen 34), and Rachel becomes pregnant again. This journey must have been trying. As the caravan approaches Bethlehem, she gives birth to her second son in great suffering (Gen 35:16–21).

Before dying, Rachel has just enough time to name her child. In Jewish tradition she symbolizes the Mother of Israel in mourning and calls her child Ben-oni, that is, "son of my sorrow." But Jacob cannot stand a name that so evokes the suffering of his wife, so he calls him Benjamin. Of Jacob's thirteen children, twelve sons and a daughter, Benjamin is the only one whom he names.

Rachel's Tomb

Rachel's death and her tomb along a road summarize her whole life. She who had suffered so much from being sterile dies giving birth to a child. She who at the beginning of her married life had ceded her place to Leah is now buried along the roadside and not at Machpelah. Rachel, who was the consolation of Jacob as an exile, becomes the consolation for all exiled people. Rachel the inconsolable (Jer 31:15) becomes the source of consolation for all generations. According to the Midrash,* she awaits the return of the last Jew to the Holy Land before finally joining Jacob in the grotto of Machpelah. She is also a consolation today for Israeli and Palestinian women who mourn at her tomb for husbands and sons lost in war.

Rachel, first woman shepherd, you still watch over your flock, giving drink without respite to the women and men who thirst for comfort.

Rachel, silent lamb, you are, like the Shikinnah, the Presence of God, both exiled and present in the midst of the people, suffering from their sufferings, vulnerable with them, many a time persecuted and humiliated, inconsolable yet also an inexhaustible source of consolation.

Rachel, sterile wife, cry out for joy, for your children are more numerous than the grains of sand of the sea . . .

Conclusion

In the course of reading these chapters of Genesis, you have perhaps been astonished, as I was, by the elements that bit by bit make the wives of the patriarchs come alive as autonomous women. The story of their lives does not devolve simply in the shadow of their husbands, as centuries of Bible reading would have us believe. That story has its own originality, its own personal choices, its own adventures.

Gaps in the Patriarchal System

Certainly in a social system based on injustice, as patriarchal society is, areas of freedom ceded to women are minimal or nearly nonexistent. We have seen in particular how traumatizing the exclusion of barren women was. In a society where only motherhood was prized, not being a mother amounted to being socially dead.

At the same time we have admitted the patriarchalism of the Bible, we have tried to show that it is possible to read these texts through another lens. Being too attached to Scripture's patriarchal cast is in a way to be its victim a second time.

We have little information about the biblical authors. However, we can suppose that they wrote in a male environment. Like every writer then, they were ineluctably marked by the patriarchal type of culture in which they lived. But, and this is what interested me, their writings also contain passages where the author seems to rise above or beyond his own thinking. The American feminist theologian Phyllis Trible considers these passages as elements that allow for a deconstruction of the text in order to permit an alternative point of view on the patriarchy. In the thread of our reading we have observed that these passages, which are actually relatively numerous, allow another approach to, another reading of the biblical text.

Because these possibilities exist within the biblical text, I think one cannot, without doing injury to God, reduce Scripture to a simple production of patriarchal culture and use this as the pretext for no longer reading it, studying it, or being inspired by it, as some women have done. Genesis contains too many texts that show women as autonomous persons, counterparts of men, for anyone to continue to make a unilateral reading.

Moreover, as Elisabeth Schüssler-Fiorenza justly points out, "God did not create or plan the patriarchy, but God created people as human beings, male and female. Woman was not given into the power of man to establish his house, his family, but it is the man who must cut the bonds with his own patriarchal family, and 'the two will become one flesh.'" And she adds that because of the use of the word "flesh," which in Greek has a very broad meaning, it would be better to translate it this way: "The two people, man and woman, partake of one human life and one common social relation because they were created equal."

Alert to God

In Genesis 12 which tells us about the beginning of the life of Abraham and his wife, we observe that Sarah, far from being only a minor companion of her husband, is a woman with her own part to play and behaves as such. Through what we have called the "messianic choice," she even becomes the central character in Abraham's story. Without her, without the boldness of her love, the promise could not have been fulfilled, and this fulfillment was possible not only because she was the mother of Isaac, but also because she was first and essentially alert to the will of God.

For these women motherhood does not in the end represent the most important element of their existence. That is true only for the patriarchal structures that consider woman solely as the means of building up a man's family.

For this reason concerning the couple Isaac and Rebekah, we have observed that despite the patriarchal structures of society, it is only the mothers who name their children, and they often take advantage of this to choose a name that denounces their condition as women. Leah did this (Gen 29:31–35), and so did Rachel, who calls her second son Ben-oni, "son of my sorrow." This is such an evident complaint about her condition as a woman that Jacob does not stand for it and immediately changes his name to Benjamin (Gen 35:18).

While it remains true that God prefers to talk to the patriarchs, we see God also speaking directly to Hagar (Gen 16:7–14; 21:17–19), and it is only to Rebekah that he confides the secret linked to the birth of her two sons

(Gen 25:22–23). God grants Isaac's prayer (Gen 25:21), but God also remembers Rachel and grants her prayer too (Gen 30:22). The matriarchs—we hope to have shown it in this book—were chosen by God expressly because of their capacity to hear God's Word and put it into practice.

Much later Jesus will say the same thing when he explains that it is not the woman who bore and suckled him that was blessed, but the one who hears the Word of God and turns it into action (Luke 11:27–28; cf. Luke 10:42). Through the course of their lives the matriarchs help us discover that what is important is not biological motherhood but being alert to God and living according to God's will, being a disciple. They teach us, in hidden but nonetheless clear ways, that the vocation of woman is to be a fulltime partner with God in the divine work of liberation.

Lexicon of the Jewish Tradition

Midrash—From the Hebrew verb "to explore/to study." Midrash is homiletical literature that consists of a vast assemblage of biblical commentaries, in a direct yet poetic style. The most important Midrash is the "Midrash Rabbah," or the Great Midrash. With legends, stories, poems, allegories, moral reflections, historical reminiscences, and take-offs on the biblical text, it explains the Pentateuch. The Midrashes were compiled between the 5th and the 12th centuries, but the collected material belongs for the most part to the Talmudic Period (see Talmud*).

Rashi—Rabbi Solomon ben Isaac, called Rashi, a French Jew (1040-1105), was a commentator on the Torah* and the Talmud.* At Troyes he founded a rabbinical school whose influence spread to Germany, southern France, and Spain.

Talmud—Formed from the Mishnah and the Gemara, Talmud is a collection of commentaries on the Torah.* The Mishnah (lit. "repetition") is the oldest rabbinical code, compiled around A.D. 200 and edited by Rabbi Judah; after the Bible it is the basic document of Judaism. The Gemara (lit. "completion") is a further commentary on it, compiled and edited around A.D. 500. There are two Talmuds: the Talmud of Jerusalem (4th c. A.D.) composed in Palestine, also called the Palestinian Talmud, and the Babylonian Talmud (5th c. A.D.), which is more developed and by itself has a normative value. The latter is the one referred to when the Talmud in general is mentioned.

Targum—Hebrew word meaning "translation." The Targums are translations of the Hebrew Bible into Aramaic. The goal of these translations is also to be an interpretation, and we find explanations, images, and stories interspersed in the biblical text.

Torah—Hebrew word meaning "Law." Torah is the assemblage of stipulations that Jewish tradition ascribes to Moses; the word designates also the first five books of the Bible, the Pentateuch.

Zohar—Literally "The Book of Splendor," the Zohar is a commentary on the Pentateuch. This is the major work of the Kabbalah, the school of thought concerned with the mystical and allegorical interpretation of the Bible practiced in certain Jewish communities in the Middle Ages. The Zohar belongs to the old Midrash,* whose form it imitates. It is traditionally attributed to Rabbi Simeon bar Yohai.

Short Bibliography

THE AUTHOR HAS LIMITED this list to some of the works in that inspired her reading.

Amado Lévy-Valensi, Eliane. *La onzième épreuve d'Abraham.* Paris, 1981.

Challier, Cathérine. *Les Matriarches.* Paris, 1985.

Eisenberg, J. and A. Abécassis. *Jacob, Rachel, Léa et les autres.* Paris, 1981.

Hayek, Michel. *Le mystère d'Ismaël.* Paris, 1964.

Munk, Élie. *La voix de la Torah, La Génèse.* Paris, 1976.

Neher, André and Renée Neher. *Histoire biblique du Peuple d'Israël.* Neuchâtel, 1982.

Quéré, France and Denys Prache. *Dis-moi, Denys, qui sont ces femmes.* Paris, 1983.

Schüssler-Fiorenza, Elisabeth. *In Memory of Her.* New York, 1985.

Vanel, Jean. *Le livre de Sara.* Paris, 1984.

Wagner, Gaston. *La justice dans l'Ancien Testament et le Coran.* Neuchâtel, 1977.

Ancient Jewish and Islamic texts that the author cites are taken chiefly from Hayek and Munk, and here are simply translated from the French.

To emphasize the continuity of God's plan, the author uses the "First Testament" to refer to the "Old," and the "Second Testament" to refer to the "New."